FROM MY STRUGGLES COMES MY STRENGTH

———

MALIK MALACHI

From My Struggles Comes My Strength

Copyright © 2026 by Malik Malachi

All rights reserved. No part of this book may be reproduced or transmitted in any form or by any means without written permission from the author.

ISBN 979-8-9987951-2-1(Paperback)

Publication Date: March 21, 2026

Contact Information

alurepublishingllc@gmail.com

www.alurepublishing.net

DEDICATION

To my wife Emily, for never doubting me.

To my brothers Guya & Alfonzo, whom I love until love is no more.

To my sister Missy, whom I miss dearly—we finally did it.

To my father, thank you for the good and the bad. I miss you.

To my mother—without you, none of this is possible. I miss you.

To my stepmother: it wasn't your egg, but you nurtured it to maturity. Thank you. I hope I have made you proud.

To my host of cousins, nieces, and nephews—thank you for being you.

To my grandchildren—remember: anyone can learn from their own mistakes, but only a wise

person learns from the mistakes of others.
I LOVE YOU ALL.

Special dedication to my Aunt Dolores Johnson and Uncle Nathaniel Davis. Thank you both for helping me become who I am.

To my sons—Malachi (RIP), William, Malik (Greg), Shawn, Hayward, Tony, and Jibriel—you are the fuel of this book. I leave you with three life lessons:

1. Your time is the most valuable thing you can give—use it well.
2. Always be true to yourself; no man serves two masters' successfully.
3. Guard, nurture, and build your spirituality, for it is your foundation—and in the end, it is the only thing that cannot be taken.

TABLE OF CONTENTS

Dedication
Preface
Today I See Colors: Part I 1
Today I See Colors: Part II 7
Insurmountable Obstacles 10
    Insurmountable Obstacles 13

Judas..15
Sneak Thief 22
Death the Future of Life 25
Why You Worried About My Vision? 31
Smile Translated in Different Language...........37
    That Smile 38

Thorn In My Side 45
33 Struggles..49
Special Thanks..53

PREFACE

Chapter one saved the Authors life and it was also marked the beginning of his healing process. Healing from child abuse, domestic violence, alcohol and drug as well as sexual abuse. No child should be forced to process issues of an adult nature it taints and distorts the mind and at some point it impedes growth and development; hence the reason some of these actions are repeated from generation after generation. Children often repeat what they see and become like the person they disliked the most. This book is not meant to blame reveal or expose anyone. The Author does not want any apologies, pity or sorrow.

To add insult to injury after working as a licensed optician for years the Author has been dealing with blindness in both eyes since 2000.

The soul purpose of this book is to heal and help others. The Author truly feels everyone who reads this book and are honest with themselves will relate to something in it. The plan is not to take the Authors path but to invoke thought so the path that is taken brakes the CYCLE. (The ultimate goal.)

Enjoy "TODAY I SEE COLORS".

"PAIN IS INEVITABLE. SUFFERING IS OPTIONAL"

HARUKI MURAKAMI

TODAY I SEE COLORS

PART I

I see colors of a time long pasted, when
everything seemed to be so dark like the day when
I was molested: Or the day my father beat me
with a monkey wrench.
I see colors
Today I see colors
I see the colors of my step-mothers face on the
morning of my twelfth birthday,
All day my mind replayed the picture of the blood
running like a waterfall.
Happy-Birthday to me.
I see colors

Today I see colors
I see the colors of a woman's tear because I
pushed her away; yet she
left me, what colors were my tears, Mom?
I see colors

Today I see colors
I see the redness of pain I would later inflict on
every living creature that dared to care.
I see colors of lewd and lascivious acts
orchestrated by me, and justified by
enmity, funded with resentment. I see colors of
the wives I never hit but neglected, abused and
misused in every-other conceivable way possible.
I see colors

Today I see colors
I see the green of money that I hoped would
define me, while I searched to control a life fueled
with greed, crime, drugs, manipulation mayhem,
and yes pain.
Wow, I see colors

Today I see colors
I see the colors of gloominess as life leaves every
life I touch. The colors
of gun shots and violence ring everywhere. I see
colors as no tears fall from
within my empty shell. I see the color of fear as
life sentences come down

like snowflakes in the midst of a storm.
I see colors

Today I see colors as I run thinking my efforts
will save my children from the
color of deaths Angel; Now I know my intent was
to save them from me! "Rest in
Peace my son".
I see colors

Today I see colors from city to city, state to state,
stash-house to stash-house,
prison to prison.
I see colors

Today I escaped from the color of death, only
to die…

The End

MALIK MALACHI

TODAY I SEE COLORS

PART II

I see the vivid colors of my future. I see the ugly colors of hate and pain get swallowed by the unconditional colors of love and self-forgiveness: As I reconcile with my inner self for having such a volatile past I see the colors of hope and promise, and I'm inspired beyond belief.

Today I see colors
I see the bright colors of compassion knowing
often times people repeat
what they know, refusing to change.

Today I see colors
I see the supreme colors of forgiveness because
bad things happen to good people sometimes,
even the sick are God's creation.

Today I see colors
I see the clear colors of integrity within my
relationships now, and the dark colors

of misogyny no longer consumes me. For once
I'm able to grow like the seed exposed to the sun.

Today I see colors
Colors of sincere joy and laughter, free to trust
and be trusted; I see the colors of irrational acts
turn rational, I see the colors of unacceptable
behavior become
acceptable, I see the colors of adversity and it
introduced me to myself what a
vibrant color I am.

Today I see colors
I see colors that no longer need to escape reality.
The evil colors that once motivated my insanity
has made peace with my past, and the colors of
recovery and healing are now finally possible.

Today I see colors
I see the colors of my blessings both large and
small. How wonderful are the colors I see when
my sons are responsible, respectful, productive
young men.

Today I see colors
I see the colors of gratitude free from shame,

colors that reject my burdens of yesterday; the anxiety of tomorrow as I begin to live in the now

Today I see colors
Colors of an intrinsic value that lives within me. I see a plethora of colors today; I see colors of my humanity have been resuscitated and my dignity is restored with flying colors.

Today I see colors
'It is not the eyes that go blind but it is the heart that refuses to see'.

God has impeccable timing and what lavish colors…

The Beginning

22:46 Qur'an

INSURMOUNTABLE OBSTACLES

That's what I've become, an insurmountable obstacle. Too often I can't get out of my own way, I am my own adversary impeaching myself before the event begins. My mind is this sinister master while my body is its obtuse slave; like the mouse falling in love with the snake, or shooting myself in the foot because I have two, or even crazier to rim-rock myself without rhyme or reason.

Day-in and day-out I strain to find a raised voice, an arched eyebrow, or that educated tongue to awaken or save me from myself, my own worst enemy. Today again, I've failed because of that insurmountable obstacle. The impish facade that's meant to placate the crowd only prolongs the crash and echo's its impact.

All of my memories seem to be linked to an unescapable reaccuring nightmare making sleep at times a horrific experience; another complication of that insurmountable obstacle, the kind that are rarely if ever depicted on the pages of books or the brightness of film.

Still I question myself, "Am I afraid to succeed; why am I a fugitive of success; is success my life long nemesis?" The answers elude me daily.

No matter where I sit, stand or lay that insurmountable Obstacle never goes astray.

INSURMOUNTABLE OBSTACLES

D-estroy	*my*	*D-reams*
E-rase	*my*	*E-xpectations*
P-oison	*my*	*P-otential*
R-elinquish	*my*	*R-eality*
E-xtract	*my*	*E-steem*
S-ubdue	*my*	*S-pirit*
S-urrender	*to*	*S-uicide*
I-ntentions	*become*	*I-llegitimate*
O-bjective	*become*	*O-blique*
N-ature	*become*	*N-egative*

This is a mental illness awareness message. That Insurmountable Obstacle
has a name, look closely; do you see it?

(The author was diagnosed with depression anxiety and PTSD*)*

JUDAS

The breach of confidence
The pre-school tattletale
The double-crossing sibling
The snitching juvenile
The adolescent rat turncoat
The promiscuous spouse
The dime-dropper on the job
The gossipmonger at church
The ultimate deceiver
The void of trust
The informer of mankind
The trickery of treason
The betrayal of everything good
The uncovering of concealed sins

To be hoodwinked, violated, bamboozled, stabbed in the back, is to be human.

Who is your Judas?

I Remember

I remember deep in the contours of my mind between consciousness and fantasy, I remember you. I remember the second our paths crossed it was like two clouds intertwined , quiet, but visible for all the world to see; summoned together by your captivating smile, filled with the grace and beauty that's visited only in dreams, admired by all but controlled by none. I remember such intimacy never to be duplicated.

I Remember

I remember the exact sensation of holding your hand for the very first time. I never knew a touch could be so meaningful, so satisfying, like making a child laugh with a small gesture or act of kindness; I remember it warms the heart.

I Remember

I remember being intoxicated with your eyes, they seem to take me to galaxies far beyond the milky way to planets discovered only by us, like I'm hallucinating with every glance! You my dear are the preamble to my addiction; you are my luxury for which I could never prove worthy. I remember that love affair that exceeded both time and space.

I Remember

I remember before meeting you my life was total chaos, I wasn't a participant in my own existence, I made the rules as situations arose. I remember my heart was cold and you ignited it by looking beyond my exterior appearance for what lurked beneath the surface. I remember you showed me how to give voice to the truth of my past and it opened doors to our future; I remember Love can sometimes achieve the impossible.

I Remember

I remember the exquisite features of your bone structure, your body carved into utter perfection, deliberately. Yes, you are my lifelong obsession! Mesmerizing is your presence, grateful is your aura, vintage is your spirit, enlightening is your intellect, tranquil is your gift, and love is your message and I remember that message. "Love me for who and what I am, please don't make me over".

I Remember

I remember every detail of that day when the sun refused to shine in our world. I felt a feeling in my heart, it was beyond pain but not yet horror, that day my mind ran like a merry-go-round with no off switch, and I remembered "The heart knows before the mind". When tragedy strikes questions follow, but all I could hear was your sweet voice in the midst saying "We are troubled and challenged in multiple ways". Today your passing remains for me a wound unhealed, a hole unfilled and a challenge unmet. I miss you from my core.

I Remember

Now many Suns and Moons have come and gone and still I remember, when I close my eyes I inhale your breathtaking fragrance, it's like your scent arrested my nose and sentenced it to life smelling only lavender and jasmine with a hint of frankincense, what bliss I remember; I could see the ghost of your former smile and again it seduced my heart without intent or regret and I remember, as I open my eyes and still I remember. Today my thoughts are not consumed with regret, but with you, and with pen in hand I wonder is it even possible to articulate a love like ours? Words seem so inadequate when trying to capture and describe my true feeling for you my dear, but I do remember…Lover –of- Mine there are dreams that visit and leave us fulfilled upon waking, and there are dreams that make life worth living, you my sweet are that dream. My life is infinitely better because of you." Thank You".

I Remember

I remember the way you attacked life with joyful abandon and sorrowful surrender. I remember you repeating with conviction "It's never to late to do the right thing". I'm trying baby, I'm trying, its extremely hard without you…

I Remember

I remember you, My dream, My companion, My lover and My friend, but more than that you are my ideal wife. You have faith in the goodness of mankind and that's God's gift to you, and you are God's gift to me. I remember when I proposed I asked "To be your husband in this life and in the next". How fortunate am I to get a double dip of you. I remember while Love can heel, it can also hurt.

I Remember

Viewing the billboards of my mind and playing and replaying the scenes from the love and life we once shared, how I cherish that time an amenity that allows me to face the tomorrows, until destiny and time meet and are struck by the meaning of life and death simultaneously and see they are one. As we shared life's chronicles so shall we share deaths odyssey.

I Remember

A blink,
A sneeze,
 A missed heart-beat,
A final exhalation and we will be reunited forever.

I LOVE YOU ENDLESSLY
IN STRENGTH AND IN STRUGGLE
IN LIFE AND IN DEATH
YOUR HUSBAND IN THIS LIFE AND IN THE NEXT

We have a symbiosis that coincide with the universe,
Who can ask for more…

YES,
I REMEMBER

SNEAK THIEF

Eyes of eternal   **G**ratitude

Eyes of undying   **L**oyalty

Eyes of enormous   **A**mbition

Eyes of spectacular   **U**nderstanding

Eyes of midnight   **C**omedy

Eyes of illuminating   **O**pinion

Eyes of elusive   **M**ystery

Eyes of dynamic   **A**chievement

At first glance you only read the eyes of
irresistible promise and strength, the eyes that
Gleam and sparkle with life and vitality, eyes of a
bright and exuberant future, but if you
look at the real message, you'll read of eyes
afflicted with a deteriorating sickness and in
immense pain: eyes that no longer look forward to
seeing the tomorrows, now they long
for the final day. You'll know the name of that
shattering disease, the one that hijacked
my sight, the disease that changed life as I knew
and enjoyed it, the disease that transformed me
from normal to abnormal, from whole to broken,
from able to disable,
from literate to illiterate, from an independent
individual who once led others to a hinderance
and bother to all. This disease stole my self-worth
and esteem then called me handicapped.

Doctors refer to this disease as the "Sneak Thief
of Vision", but I saw it coming from
far far away and couldn't allude or escape its
grasp, nothing would change or disrupt
the course of this extremely focused disease.

Surgery after Surgery and the only thing was clear was, this was not a test it was an
Actual Emergency.

This disease seized my sight like termites in a wooden house, treatment was to no avail
Because the foundation (Optical Nerve) was only a shadow of its former self. Life can be
a cruel teacher, sometimes you get the test before you get the lesson.

After years of being assaulted by this militant disease and its destruction, my eyes are no longer the windows to my soul. But from turbulence, trauma and suffering came the path to my humility.

Gratitude was born when my spiritual awareness surfaced
Loyalty came easy once I could distinguish truth from falsehood
Ambition taught me how to access, improvise, adapt and overcome
Understanding and knowing my limitations keep me sane and grounded

Comedy and laughter replace anger and frustration with a fresh perspective
Opinions from family and trusted friends help avoid some setbacks and obstacles
Mystery can be dangerous because in our darkest hours our secrets eat us alive
Achievement is to look back into the sand and see the footsteps of your creator and
obtain instant humility by his grace and mercy.

My father once told me "Courage is not the absence of fear but is the ability to continue
In the face of it."
I can now comprehend how something which once seemed like a major disaster turned out to be a blessing.

"No soul shall bare a burden more than it can carry" Qur'an 2;287

THE THIEF HAS TAKEN MY SIGHT, BUT GOD HAS ENHANCED MY ABILITY TO SEE...

DEATH THE FUTURE OF LIFE"

Dead are not truly dead until they are forgotten.

Eternal dwelling place of flesh and bone, from the dirt we came, to the dirt we shall return.

Anonymous are the souls, unique is the road traveled, and guaranteed is the experience.

Truth is undeniable, sometimes unbelievable but always present, such as life and death.

Harmony between life and death surrender to each-other, while visiting the infinite womb of mercy both are helpless.

Death the Future of Life

Weather Agnostic, Atheist, Baptist, Buddhist, Catholic, Hindu, Jewish, Muslim, Pagan, Proestent or Satan worshipper all shall taste death regardless of color, creed or sexual orientation.

Murder, Suicide, Cardiovascular disease, Decapitation, Drug overdose, Brain Aneurysm, Cancer, Old age, Car crash, Cirrhosis, Malnutrition or Crib death all remind us constantly the clock that ticks belongs to neither you nor I; No speeding paramedics will out-run that clock, so predictable yet mysterious, no telepathic lunatic will postpone, stop or alter its fate. No one keeps the death angel waiting. Rigor-Mortis is not a choice, it's a destiny, yet death looks good on some, as if time has granted them a suspended sentence.

Death is always something abstract and foreign until it hits home, then do we notice how selfish we can be. We cry because we are going to miss that person, because they left us, or we won't see them, touch them or spend time with them. We say things like "They're in a better place" to appease ourselves, for no one among the living truly knows. Sometimes we'll become angry with God or even at the deceased loved-one; we question them "why take him or her, you should have taken me instead" or "why did you leave me, if you loved me you wouldn't have left me, alone?" It's really hard to deal with grief, it often causes misplaced anger and obviously it leaves a void. The pain is so enormous, some people never recover completely. When death speaks no creation can remain unmoved, sorrow floods the hearts and soul of every living creature.

Death the Future of Life

From pediatric to geriatric, death exist on every level at every age yet it's never an easy pill to swallow. We see only a small part of the entire scene, so simplistic and yet so intricate. Maybe one life is a punishment for another, or maybe life is the punishment and death the reward? Something to ponder, but worry not the answer will be revealed in life's future.

Come one, Come all, just as the Sun, Moon and Stars have an appointed date and time, so shall we; may we shine as bright until that day.

IF DEATH IS THE FUTURE OF LIFE
LIFE IS THE HISTORY OF DEATH

Once chosen by life, nothing is surer then death.

Live right
Die
Correct

REFERENCE: Genesis 3:19 Bible

WHY YOU WORRIED ABOUT MY VISION?

Can you see the hungry children in your community, the ones that go to bed in pain from hunger almost every night? Are your children friends with a hungry child? Do you Know?

Can you see what your children are doing when you're not around; who are they hanging out with what are they eating, drinking or smoking? Do you know?

How are things in school? Are you an active parent? Can you name child's teachers?
Do they have Your cell number and/or e-mail address, do you answer when they call or question when they don't, what was the last science project? Do you know?

Is your child allowed to live in a video game or on the cell phone 24/7? Are they aware
of the atrocities going on in the world today and

how will it affect them and their future? Do you know?

Are your children sexually active and if so with whom? Do you know? Are you the parent of
A bully, or is your child the one bullied? Do you know?

Have you explained to your child the ramifications of their actions dealing with but not limited to drugs, sex, drinking, texting and driving, drinking and driving bad company, Trying to fit in etc. etc. How will they respond when the time comes? Do you know?

If you want to know what I see, first look at unemployment and homelessness both far beyond past limits and rising. Big cities have filed bankruptcy, and you worry about my
vision, look at the vision of your children and grandchildren; it's a thin line between the Unemployed, the employed and the employer, or the homeowner, and the homeless.
Freedom is not free; one bad choice and destiny can become clear. That's what I see!

Look at the drug epidemic, a worldwide crisis, not
only are our urban youth lost to their
environments but the upper- and middle-class
youth are meth and smack addicts, selling
Their bodies for pennies and their souls for less.
That's what I see!

I see inner city schools around the country being
closed everyday while prisons are continuously
being opened. The congressional crooks in
Washington DC vote incarceration
over education all in the name of budget cuts; yet
education is cheaper; so, what's the
real reason? That which is done in the dark shall
one day come to light. That's what I see.

Large companies moving to third-world countries
for cheap labor and less taxes, if any.
The so-called American dream has crossed the
border; the land of milk and honey has
surrendered to the bitterness of greed and men.
That's what I see.

I see mass killing become an everyday
occurrence, from elementary school to middle

And high school, even colleges. To send your child to school on Monday to seek an education. And plan their funeral on Friday. How dare you worry about what I see.

I see the workplace turn into a war zone, for no good reason. The elderly are afraid to leave the house or stay at home for fear of bullets coming through the walls. Now tell me again why are you worrying about what I see?

Animals are snatching our young girls off the streets forcing them into human trafficking
And you have the time to be concerned about how much I can see.

Mental illness is at an all-time high and mental hospital are quietly closing at an alarming rate; negating much needed treatment and medications that are forgotten by the mentally
ill and ignored by the mental-health world until tragedy strikes; then who's sanity should be questioned? Blame is easily given but seldom taken. That's what I see.

I see technology rob the one- on- one social skills of the present and future generations, they communicate only with technology making us slaves to our own advancement.
Watch when the new apple technology come out people will camp-out all night and even go into debt to keep up with the master. That's what I see.

I see gangs spread like chicken pox in a orphanage, they have become conglomerates in the drug trade as well as prostitution and guns, using sex and fun for appetizers to seduce the young and uninformed, ambushing them into a nefarious world full of evil deeds and reckless actions. That's what I see.

I see the pharmaceutical administration earn billion upon billions of dollars monthly with medications that help high cholesterol, but its side effects harm the respiratory system or give you hypertension so we can't win for losing here's a pill for everything as long as you pay the co-payment. That's what I see.

Next time you see me waiting to cross the street before you become fixated on my vision or lack of, remember this "It's not good to concern yourself with other people's affairs because in the process you short change yourself, and you deserve more" That's what I know.

If you want to know about my disease, ask and I'll be happy to educate you about it, but don't second guess my sight with your eyes because that makes you blind with ignorance, and I may be the one hit as a result.

Now you know what I see, don't worry about what I can't see.

Keep your eyes on the prize,
You and yours.

The blind giving you sight…

SMILE TRANSLATED IN DIFFERENT LANGUAGE

Language	Word	Transliteration/ Gender
Arabic	ابْتِسَ	ibtisāma
Chinese (Mandarin)	微笑	wēixiào
French	sourire	(m)
German	Lächeln	(n)
Italian	sorriso	(m)
Japanese	ほほ笑み	hohoemi
Korean	미소	miso
Portuguese	sorriso	(m)
Russian	улыбка	ulibka
Spanish	sonrisa	(f)
Swedish	leende	(n)
Vietnamese	nụ cười	

THAT SMILE

I look out the window and search the deep blue sky for that smile,
among the breathtaking clouds within its heavenly shades of blue-
silver and reddish-oranges, I look for you that magnanimous smile.

That Smile

I long for that smile as the sun peeks over the eastern horizon in its
quest to lighten, nurture and reveal Gods creation, I'm in awe as I
gasp at the sight of such wonderment, still I am empty save that remarkable smile.

That Smile

That smile is the home of my essence, my being, my special purpose.
Every second I'm in pursuit of that smile.
Moment after moment
the longing becomes more intense, more

deliberate almost
unbearable. As the hours pass the anxieties
multiply beyond even
gravity's reach. That smile, that tumultuous smile.

That Smile

My days and nights are solicited with dreams of that smile, how
Sumptuous and blissful, the mere image of that smile supersedes
My mind's most elaborate fantasy. That unquestionable smile answers to no man or creation.

That Smile

That beautiful smile is the choreographer that dictates every beat of my heart, the GPS to my bloodstream and its swift movements from my heart to my brain and all the vital organs therein. How spectacular and stimulating, such proficiency is generated without the slightest effort. That everlasting smile knows no bounds or limitations.

That Smile

That smile is the utensil I use to maintain survival, overcome
obstacles and keep peace within my own troubled existence.
That illustrious smile restores faith and hope were humanity
has failed.

That Smile

That smile has the charisma that could charm the heat from the sun
The oxygen from the air and the calm from the ocean, instantly. That
Smile without equivalent or substitute speaks volumes to those who
seek its company, and what magnificent company to have, that
Legendary smile.

That Smile

Provides vision for the future. That smile is inspiration for the
present. That smile is clarity of the past.

That Smile

Liberates, relieves and soothes

That Smile

Relaxes. Satisfies and improves

That Smile

Gives pleasure repeatedly because that smile breathes life into
every soul

That Smile

Sparkles and luminates, it generates a euphoria that's second to
none. There's no greater intimacy or adventure and I Thank You for
the miracle of that unforgettable smile.

That Smile has no beginning nor end for that smile is my eternal
Friend…

FROM MY STRUGGLES COMES MY STRENGTH

SMILE.

THEY ARE THE REASON WHY I SMILE

THORN IN MY SIDE

Some have heard of you …thorn in my side
You are bound to me and my family
I can feel your presence when you come and when you leave, sometimes I can't feel your presence at all
Thorn in my side.. That's what you are!

I heard that you visit some of your prey daily to manipulate and tear their lives apart
Some you don't visit as frequently but the wait is terrifying
Knowing you can come without any invitation
Thorn in my side …that's what you are!

The mixed emotions i feel when you creep into my life
Sometimes i can see you from afar because you change my surroundings
Your presence is deceiving with the brightness you bring, only to later to bring bitter darkness and a bad taste in my mouth.
Thorn in my side…. That's what you are!

The pain, you bring me can sometimes be devastating
I've heard about you, some say you give them power; electrifying some might even say but to others you drain them, mind body and soul
You used to bring me fear that this visit may be my last
How will my family accept this …. Leaving me lifeless with no remorse
You are not mines to keep
You have so many names
So much strength to manipulate my mind
To make my body do exactly what you'd have it to do |I pray to god to release me from your ugly snares that bind me
You no longer have power over me and my family!
Thorn in my side… that's what you are!

Today I call you out!
Epilepsy, you have no more control in my life
I am freed of your holds, the fears and your power
I will live and not die
Peace and joy to live no longer bound is what

FROM MY STRUGGLES COMES MY STRENGTH

I have
Thorn in my side … that's what you were

EMILY MUHAMMAD

33 STRUGGLES

1. I struggle to see the lessons of yesterday, the experiences of today, and the hope for tomorrow.

2. I struggle to keep impurities out of my body as well as my thinking.

3. I struggle not to discriminate against others because only yesterday I was discriminated against.

4. I struggle to think with my head and not my heart and I struggle to love with my heart and not my head.

5. I struggle never to allow mass suffering to become normal in my thinking.

6. I struggle for my most rational moments to shine in my most trying times.

7. I struggle to find happiness in a world full of greed and discontent; happiness is an inside job. (Find yours.)

8. I struggle to be at war with my vices and at peace with my neighbors.

9. I struggle to control my anger so I'm not haunted by it's aftermath.

10. I struggle to forgive my love ones while the my wounds are still raw, true forgiveness is often sought but rarely given.

11. I struggle to advise when asked based on wisdom not emotions.

12. I struggle to trust even when to distrust appears easier and less painful.

13. I struggle to fight for that which is right, even when the odds are against me.

14. I struggle to embrace progress rather than perfection.

15. I struggle to be humble when my ego is at its highest point.

16. I struggle to know when to lead and when to follow.

17. I struggle to reinvent myself into the man I was meant to be.

18. I struggle to always do the right thing when nobody is watching; the true test.

19. I struggle not to confuse war with progress; in war there are no winners.

20. I struggle to be a better husband, father, and human being; A life- long struggle.

21. I struggle to stay focused, diligent and persistent in all life's endeavors.

22. I struggle to walk by faith not by sight. Vision often taints perception and twist reality.

23. I struggle to add substance to every life my life touches.

24. I struggle to speak for those without a voice until they are able to speak for themselves.

25. I struggle to forgive me enemies while never forgetting their names.

26. I struggle to say 'NO' regardless of how much the devil in me says 'YES'.

27. I struggle to give so that I may give more tomorrow.

28. I struggle to never hate anyone, for hate corrupts morals, poisons the heart and kills the soul.

29. I struggle to never put someone else down to show how high I am.

30. I struggle not to procrastinate for tomorrow is promised to no one.

31. I struggle to judge based on actions not words. A person will make the mouth say anything.

32. I struggle not to let someone else's actions change who I am.

33. I struggle to always be grateful and remember where all my blessings, large and small come from.

SPECIAL THANKS

Library for the blind New York

Enoch Pratt Library MD

Library of Zebulon NC

library for the Greensboro NC

free library of Philadelphia PA

La Retama Central library Corpus Chisti TX

Central Library of Atlanta GA

Queens library of South Ozone Park NY

Library of eastern shore MD

Wicomico County detention center

For your help with my research and your patience with me.

To my I.T. team Jessica and Brianna Thank you

Finally, thank you to City Block Health of Greensboro. Without you, this story could be very different